This dictionary of Latin Legal Terms can serve as an important resource for a practicing attorney, an aspiring/current law student, or anyone who is looking to learn more about the derivative sources for a majority of the legal concepts that govern Common Law Jurisdictions.

A..

B..

C..

D..

E..

F..

G..

H..

I..

J..

L..

M...

N..

O..

P..

Q..

R..

S..

T..

U..

V..

A vinculo matrimonii - From the bond of matrimony.

Ab extra - From outside.

Ab initio - From the beginning.

Absoluta sententia expositore non indiget - An absolute judgment needs no expositor.

Abundans cautela non nocet - Abundant caution does no harm.

Accessorium non ducit sed sequitur suum principale - An accessory does not draw, but follows its principal.

Accessorius sequitur - One who is an accessory to the crime cannot be guilty of a more serious crime than the principal offender.

Acta exteriora iudicant interiora secreta - Outward acts indicate the inward intent.

Actio non accrevit infra sex annos - The action has not accrued within six years.

Actio non datur non damnificato - An action is not given to one who is not injured.

Actio personalis moritur cum persona - A personal action dies with the person.

Actiones legis - Law suits.

Actori incumbit onus probandi - The burden of proof lies on the plaintiff.

Actus nemini facit injuriam - The act of the law does no one wrong.

Actus non facit reum nisi mens sit rea - The act does not make one guilty unless there be a criminal intent.

Actus reus - A guilty deed or act.

Ad ea quae frequentius acciduunt jura adaptantur - The laws are adapted to those cases which occur more frequently.

Ad hoc - For this purpose.

Ad infinitum - Forever, without limit, to infinity.

Ad perpetuam rei memoriam - For a perpetual memorial of the matter.

Ad quaestionem facti non respondent judices; ad quaestionem legis non respondent juratores - The judges do not answer to a question of fact; the jury do not answer to a question of Law.

Aedificare in tuo proprio solo non licet quod alteri noceat - It is not lawful to build on one's own land what may be injurious to another.

Aequitas legem sequitur - Equity follows the law.

Aequitas nunquam contravenit legem - Equity never contradicts the law.

Alibi - At another place, elsewhere.

Alienatio rei praefertur juri accrescendi - Alienation is preferred by law rather than accumulation.

Aliunde - From elsewhere, or, from a different source

Allegans contraria non est audiendus - One making contradictory statements is not to be heard.

Allegans suam turpitudinem non est audiendus - One alleging his own infamy is not to be heard.

Allegatio contra factum non est admittenda - An allegation contrary to a deed is not to be heard.

Ambiguitas contra stipulatorem est - An ambiguity is most strongly construed against the party using it.

Ambiguitas verborum patens nulla verificatione excluditur - A patent ambiguity is never helped by averment.

Amicus curiae - A friend of the Court.

Angliae jura in omni casu libertati dant favorem - The laws of England are favorable in every case to liberty.

Animo furandi - With an intention of stealing.

Animo testandi - With an intention of making a will.

Annus luctus - The year of mourning.

Ante - Before.

Aqua currit et debet currere, ut currere solebat - Water runs and ought to run.

Arbitrium est judicium - An award is a judgment.

Arbor dum crescit; lignum cum crescere nescit - A tree while it grows, wood when it cannot grow.

Argumentum ab auctoritate fortissimum est in lege - An argument drawn from authority is the strongest in law.

Argumentum ab impossibilii plurimum valet in lege - An argument from impossibility is very strong in law.

Argumentum ad hominem - An argument directed a the person.

Argumentum ad ignoratiam - An argument based upon ignorance (i.e. of one's adversary).

Arma in armatos sumere jura sinunt - The laws permit the taking up of arms against the armed.

Assentio mentium - The meeting of minds, i.e. mutual assent.

Assignatus utitur jure auctoris - An assignee is clothed with rights of his assignor.

Audi alteram partem - Hear the other side.

Aula regis - The King's Court.

B

Benignior sententia in verbis generalibus seu dubiis est preferenda - The more favorable construction is to be placed on general or doubtful words.

Bis dat qui cito dat - He gives (pays) twice who pays promptly.

Bona fide - Sincere, in good faith

Bona vacantia - Goods without an owner

Boni judicis est ampliare jurisdictionem - It is the part of a good judge to enlarge his jurisdiction, i.e. remedial authority.

Boni judicis est judicium sine dilatione mandare executioni - It is the duty of a good judge to cause execution to issue on a judgment without delay.

Boni judicis lites dirimere est - It is the duty of a good judge to prevent litigation.

Bonus judex secundum aequum et bonum judicat et aequitatem stricto juri praefert - A good judge decides according to justice and right and prefers equity to strict law.

Breve judiciale non cadit pro defectu formae - A judicial writing does not fail through defect of form.

C

Cadit quaestio - The matter admits of no further argument.

Cassetur billa (breve) - Let the writ be quashed.

Casus fortuitus non est spectandus; et nemo tenetur divinare - A fortuitous event is not to be foreseen and no person is bound to divine it.

Catalla reputantur inter minima in lege - Chattels are considered in law among the minor things.

Causa proxima, non remota spectatur - The immediate, and not the remote cause is to be considered.

Caveat emptor - Let the purchaser beware.

Caveat venditor - Let the seller beware.

Cepi corpus et est languidum - I have taken the body and the prisoner is sick.

Cepi corpus et paratum habeo - I have taken the body and have it ready.

Ceteris paribus - Other things being equal.

Consensu - Unanimously or, by general consent.

Consensus ad idem - Agreement as to the same things.

Consuetudo loci observanda est - The custom of the place is to be observed.

Contemporanea expositio est optima et fortissima in lege - A contemporaneous exposition is best and most powerful in law.

Contra - To the contrary.

Contra bonos mores - Against good morals.

Contra non valentem agere nulla currit praescriptio - No prescription runs against a person not able to act.

Contractus est quasi actus contra actum - A contract is an act as it were against an act.

Conventio et modus vincunt legem - A contract and agreement overcome the law.

Conventio privatorum non potest publico juri derogare - An agreement of private persons cannot derogate from public right.

Coram Domino Rege - In the presence of our Lord the King.

Coram non judice - Before one who is not a judge.

Corpus - Body.

Corpus delicti - The body, i.e. the gist of crime.

Corpus humanum non recipit aestimationem - A human body is not susceptible of appraisement.

Crescente malitia crescere debet et poena - Vice increasing, punishment ought also to increase.

Crimen omnia ex se nata vitiat - Crime vitiates every thing, which springs from it.

Crimen trahit personam - The crime carries the person.

Cujus est dare, ejus est disponere - He who has a right to give has the right to dispose of the gift.

Cujus est solum, ejus est usque ad coelam; et ad inferos - He who owns the soil owns it up to the sky; and to its depth.

Cum duo inter se pugnantia reperiuntur in testamentis ultimum ratum est - When two things repugnant to each other are found in a will, the last is to be confirmed.

Cursus curiae est lex curiae - The practice of the court is the law of the court.

Custos morum - A guardian of morals.

D

Damnum sine injuria - damage without legal injury.

De bonis asportatis - Of goods carried away.

De bonis non administratis - Of goods not administered.

De die in diem - From day to day.

De facto - In fact.

De futuro - In the future.

De integro - As regards the whole.

De jure - Rightful, by right.

De minimis lex non curat - The law does not notice trifling matters.

De novo - Starting afresh.

Debile fundamentum fallit opus - Where there is a weak foundation, the work fails.

Debita sequuntur personam debitoria - Debts follow the person of the debtor.

Debitor non praesumitur donare - A debtor is not presumed to make a gift.

Debitum et contractus sunt nullius loci - Debt and contract are of no particular place.

Debitum in praesenti, solvendum in futuro - A present debt is to be discharged in the future.

Delegata potestas non potest delegari - A delegated authority cannot be again delegated.

Derivativa potestas non potest esse major primitiva - The power which is derived cannot be greater than that from which it is derived.

Deus solus haeredem facere potest, non homo - God alone, not man, can make an heir.

Dies Dominicus non est juridicus - Sunday is not a day in law.

Discretio est discernere per legem quid sit justum - Discretion is to discern through law what is just.

Doli incapax - Incapable of crime.

Dominium - Ownership.

Domus sua cuique est tutissimum refugium - Every mans house is his safest refuge.

Dona clandestina sunt semper suspiciosa - Clandestine gifts are always suspicious.

Dormiunt leges aliquando, nunquam moriuntur - The laws sometimes sleep, but never die.

Doti lex favet; praemium pudoris est; ideo parcatur - The law favors dower; it is the reward of chastity, therefore let it be preserved.

Dubitante - Doubting the correctness of the decision.

Duo non possunt in solido unam rem possidere - Two cannot possess one thing each in entirety.

E

Ei incumbit probatio qui - The onus of proving a fact rests upon the man.

Ei incumbit probatio qui dicit, non qui negat - The burden of the proof lies upon him who affirms, not he who denies.

Error, qui non resistitur approbatur - An error not resisted is approved.

Et cetera - Other things of that type.

Ex cathedra - With official authority.

Ex concessis - In view of what has already been accepted/

Ex dolo malo actio non oritur - A right of action cannot arise out of fraud.

Ex facie - On the fact of it.

Ex gratia - Out of kindness, voluntary.

Ex nihilo nil fit - From nothing nothing comes.

Ex nudo pacto actio non oritur - No action arises on a contract without a consideration.

Ex parte - Proceeding brought by one person in the absence of another.

Ex post facto - By reason of a subsequent act.

Ex praecedentibus et consequentibus optima fit interpretatio - The best interpretation is made from things preceding and following.

Ex turpi causa non oritur actio - No action arises on an immoral contract.

Exceptio probat regulam - An exception proves the rule.

Executio est executio juris secundum judicium - Execution is the fulfillment of the law in accordance with the judgment.

Executio est finis et fructus legis - An execution is the end and the fruit of the law.

Executio legis non habet injuriam - Execution of the law does no injury.

Extra legem positus est civiliter mortuus - One out of the pale of the law (i.e. an outlaw) is civilly dead.

F

Faciendum - Something which is to be done.

Factum - An act or deed.

Facultas probationum non est angustanda - The right of offering proof is not to be narrowed.

Falsa demonstratio non nocet - A false description does not vitiate.

Fatetur facinus qui judicium fugit - He who flees judgment confesses his guilt.

Felix qui potuit rerum cognoscere causas - Happy is he who has been able to understand the causes of things.

Felonia implicatur in qualibet proditione - Felony is implied in every treason.

Festinatio justitiae est noverca infortunii - The hurrying of justice is the stepmother of misfortune.

Fictio cedit veritati; fictio juris non est, ubi veritas - Fiction yields to truth. Where truth is, fiction of law does not exist.

Fides servanda est - Good faith is to be preserved.

Fieri facias (abreviated fi. fa.) - That you cause to be made.

Filiatio non potest probari - Filiation cannot be proved.

Firmior et potentior est operatio legis quam dispositio hominis - The operation of law is firmer and more powerful than the will of man.

Forma legalis forma essentialis est - Legal form is essential form.

Fortior est custodia legis quam hominis - The custody of the law is stronger than that of man.

Fractionem diei non recipit lex - The law does not regard a fraction of a day.

Fraus est celare fraudem - It is a fraud to conceal a fraud.

Fraus est odiosa et non praesumenda - Fraud is odious and is not to be presumed.

Fraus et jus nunquam cohabitant - Fraud and justice never dwell together.

Fructus naturales - Vegetation which grows naturally without cultivation.

Frustra probatur quod probatum non relevat - That is proved in vain which when proved is not relevant.

Furor contrahi matrimonium non sinit, quia consensus opus est - Insanity prevents marriage from being contracted because consent is needed.

G

Generale nihil certum implicat - A general expression implies nothing certain.

Generalia praecedunt, specialia sequuntur - Things general precede, things special follow.

Generalia specialibus non derogant - Things general do not derogate from things special.

Generalis regula generaliter est intelligenda - A general rule is to be generally understood.

Gravius est divinam quam temporalem laedere majestatem - It is more serious to hurt divine than temporal majesty.

Habeas corpus - That you have the body.

Habemus optimum testem confitentem reum - We have the best witness, a confessing defendant.

Haeredem est nomen collectum - Heir is a collective name.

Haeres est nomen juris, filius est nomen naturae - Heir is a term of law, son, one of nature.

Haeres legitimus est quem nuptiae demonstrant - He is the lawful heir whom the marriage indicates.

Homo vocabulum est naturae; persona juris civilis - Man is a term of nature, person of the civil law.

I

Id est (i.e) - That is.

Id quod commune est, nostrum esse dicitur - That which is common is said to be ours.

Idem - The same person or thing.

Idem nihil dicere et insufficienter dicere est - It is the same to say nothing as not to say enough.

Ignorantia facti excusat, ignorantia juris non excusat - Ignorance of fact excuses, ignorance of law does not excuse.

Imperium in imperio - A sovereignty within a sovereignty.

Impotentia excusat legem - Impossibility is an excuse in the law.

Impunitas semper ad deteriora invitat - Impunity always leads to greater crimes.

In aequali jure melior est conditio possidentis - When the parties have equal rights, the condition of the possessor is better.

In alta proditione nullus potest esse acessorius; sed principalis solum modo - In high treason no one can be an accessory; but a principal only.

In Anglia non est interregnum - In England there is no interregnum.

In camera - In private.

In casu extremae necessitatis omnia sunt communia - In a case of extreme necessity everything is common.

In criminalibus probationes debent esse luce clariores - In criminal cases the proofs ought to be cleared than the light.

In curia domini regis, ipse in propria persona jura discernit - In the Kings Court, the King himself in his own person dispenses justice.

In delicto - At fault.

In esse - In existence.

In extenso - At full length.

In fictione legis aequitas existit - A legal fiction is consistent with equity.

In foro conscientiae - In the forum of conscience.

In futoro - In the future.

In jure non remota causa sed proxima spectatur - In law not the remote but the proximate cause is looked at.

In limine - At the outset, on the threshold.

In loco parentis - In place of the parent.

In mortua manu - In a dead hand.

In novo casu novum remedium apponendum est - In a new case a new remedy is to be applied.

In omni re nascitur res quae ipsam rem exterminat - In everything is born that which destroys the thing itself.

In omnibus - In every respect.

In pari delicto potior est conditio possidentis - When the parties are equally in the wrong the condition of the possessor is better.

In personam - Against the person.

In pleno - In full.

In quo quis delinquit in eo de jure est puniendus - In whatever thing one offends in that he is to be punished according to law.

In re dubia magis inficiatio quam affirmatio intelligenda - In a doubtful matter the negative is to be understood rather than the affirmative.

In republica maxime conservanda sunt jura belli - In a State the laws of war are to be especially observed.

In situ - In its place.

In terrorem - As a warning or deterrent.

In testamentis plenius testatoris intentionem scrutamur - In wills we seek diligently the intention of the testator.

In traditionibus scriptorum non quod dictum est, sed quod gestum est, inspicitur - In the delivery of writings (deeds), not what is said but what is done is to be considered.

In verbis, non verba sed res et ratio quaerenda est - In words, not words, but the thing and the meaning are to be inquired into.

Indicia - Marks, signs.

Injuria non excusat injuriam - A wrong does not excuse a wrong.

Intentio inservire debet legibus, non leges intentioni - Intention ought to be subservient to the laws, not the laws to the intention.

Inter alia - Amongst other things.

Interest reipublicae res judicatas non rescindi - It is in the interest of the State that things adjudged be not rescinded.

Interest reipublicae suprema hominum testamenta rata haberi - It is in the interest of the State that mens last wills be sustained.

Interest reipublicae ut quilibet re sua bene utatur - It is in the interest of the State that every one use properly his own property.

Interest reipublicase ut sit finis litium - It is in the interest of the State that there be an end to litigation.

Interim - Temporary, in the meanwhile.

Interpretare et concordare leges legibus est optimus interpretandi modus - To interpret and harmonize laws is the best method of interpretation.

Interpretatio fienda est ut res magis valeat quam pereat - Such a construction is to be made that the thing may have effect rather than it should fail.

Interruptio multiplex non tollit praescriptionem semel obtentam - Repeated interruption does not defeat a prescription once obtained.

Invito beneficium non datur - A benefit is not conferred upon one against his consent.

Ipsissima verba - The very words of a speaker.

Ipso facto - By that very fact.

Ira furor brevis est - Anger is brief insanity.

Iter arma leges silent - In war the laws are silent.

J

Judex est lex loquens - A judge is the law speaking.

Judex non potest esse testis in propira causa - A judge cannot be witness in his own cause.

Judex non potest injuriam sibi datam punire - A judge cannon punish a wrong done to himself.

Judex non reddit plus quam quod petens ipse requirit - A judge does not give more than the plaintiff himself demands.

Judiciis posterioribus fides est adhibenda - Faith must be given to later decisions.

Judicis est judicare secundum allegata et probata - It is the duty of a judge to decide according to the allegations and the proofs.

Judicium non debet esse illusorium, suum effectum habere debet - A judgment ought not to be illusory; it ought to have its proper effect.

Juduces non tenentur exprimere causam sententiae suae - Judges are not bound to explain the reason of their judgment.

Jura naturae sunt immutabilia - The laws of nature are immutable.

Jura publica anteferenda privatis juribus - Public rights are to be preferred to private rights.

Juramentum est indivisibile et non est admittendum in parte verum et in parte falsum - An oath is indivisible and it is not to be held partly true and partly false.

Jurare est Deum in testem vocare, et est actus divini cultus - To swear is to call God to witness and is an act of divine worship.

Jus - A right that is recognised in law.

Jus accrescendi praefertur oneribus - The right of survivorship is preferred to incumbrances.

Jus ad rem; jus in re - A right to a thing; a right in a thing.

Jus dicere, non jus dare - To declare the law, not to make the law.

Jus est norma recti; et quicquid est contra normam recti est injuria - The law is a rule of right; and whatever is contrary to a rule of right is an injury.

Jus naturale - Natural justice.

Jus naturale est quod apud omnes homines eandem habet potentiam - Natural right is that which has the same force among all men.

Jus scriptum aut non scriptum - The written law or the unwritten law.

Jusjurandum inter alios factum nec nocere nec prodesse debet - An oath made between third parties ought neither to hurt nor profit.

Justitia est duplec; severe puniens et vere praeveniens - Justice is two-fold; severely punishing and in reality prohibiting (offences).

Justitia firmatur solium - The throne is established by justice.

Justitia nemini neganda est - Justice is to be denied to no one.

L

Leges posteriores priores contrarias abrogant - Subsequent laws repeal prior conflicting ones.

Legibus sumptis desinentibus legibus naturae utendum est - When laws imposed by the State fail, we must use the laws of nature.

Lex aliquando sequitur aequitatem - The law sometimes follows equity.

Lex citius tolerare vult privatum damnum quam publicum malum - The law would rather tolerate a private injury than a public evil.

Lex dabit remedium - The law will give a remedy.

Lex dilationes abhorret - The law abhors delays.

Lex est judicum tutissimus ductor - The law is the safest guide for judges.

Lex est sanctio sancta jubens honesta et prohibens contraria - The law is a sacred sanction, commanding what is right and prohibiting the contrary.

Lex indendit vicinum vicini facta scire - The law presumes that one neighbor knows the acts of another.

Lex necessitatis est lex temporis i.e. instantis - The law of necessity is the law of time, that is time present.

Lex neminem cogit ad vana seu impossiblia - The law compels no one to do vain or impossible things.

Lex nil frustra facit - The law does nothing in vain.

Lex non a rege est violanda - The law must not be violated even by the King.

Lex non deficere potest in justitia exhibenda - The law cannot fail in dispensing justice.

Lex non novit patrem, nec matrem; solam veritatem - The law does not know neither father nor mother, only the truth.

Lex non oritur ex injuria - The law does not arise from a mere injury.

Lex non requirit verificari quod apparet curiae - The law does not require that to be proved which is apparent to the Court.

Lex non favet delicatorum votis - The law does not favor the wishes of the dainty.

Lex plus laudatur quando ratione probatur - The law is the more praised when it is supported by reason.

Lex prospicit not respicit - The law looks forwared, not backward.

Lex punit mendaciam - The law punishes falsehood.

Lex rejicit superflua, pugnatia, incongrua - The law rejects superfluous, contradictory and incongruous things.

Lex spectat naturae ordinem - The law regards the order of nature.

Lex succurrit ignoranti - The law succors the ignorant.

Lex tutissima cassis, sub clypeo legis nemo decipitur - Law is the safest helmet; under the shield of the law no one is deceived.

Lex uno ore omnes alloquitur - The law speaks to all through one mouth.

Longa possessio est pacis jus - Long possession is the law of peace.

Longa possessio parit jus possidendi et tollit actionem vero domino - Long possession produces the right of possession and takes away from the true owner his action.

Magister rerum usus; magistra rerum experientia - Use is the master of things; experience is the mistress of things.

Major continet in se minus - The greater contains the less.

Majus est delictum se ipsum occidere quam alium - It is a greater crime to kill ones self than another.

Mala fide - In bad faith.

Mala grammatica non vitiat chartam - Bad grammar does not vitiate a deed.

Mala in se - Bad in themselves.

Mala prohibita - Crimes prohibited.

Malitia supplet aesatem - Malice supplies age.

Malo animo - With evil intent.

Mandamus - We command.

Maximus magister erroris populus est - The people are the greatest master of error.

Melior est conditio possidentis, ubi neuter jus habet - Better is the condition of the possessor where neither of the two has the right.

Melior testatoris in testamentis spectanda est - In wills the intention of a testator is to be regarded.

Meliorem conditionem suam facere potest minor deteriorem nequaquam - A minor can make his position better, never worse.

Mens rea - Guilty state of mind.

Mentiri est contra mentem ire - To lie is to act against the mind.

Merito beneficium legis amittit, qui legem ipsam subvertere intendit - He justly loses the benefit of the law who seeks to infringe the law.

Minatur innocentibus qui parcit nocentibus - He threatens the innocent who spares the guilty.

Misera est servitus, ubi jus est vagum aut incertum - It is a miserable slavery where the law is vague or uncertain.

Mors dicitur ultimum supplicium - Death is called the extreme penalty.

Muilta exercitatione facilius quam regulis percipies - You will perceive many things more easily by experience than by rules.

N

Nam nemo haeres viventis - For no one is an heir of a living person.

Naturae vis maxima est - The force of nature is the greatest.

Necessitas inducit privilegium quoad jura privata - With respect to private rights necessity induces privilege.

Necessitas non habet legem - Necessity has no law.

Necessitas publica est major quam privata - Public necessity is greater than private necessity.

Negligentia semper habet infortuniam comitem - Negligence always has misfortune for a companion.

Nemo admittendus est inhabilitare se ipsum - No one is allowed to incapacitate himself.

Nemo bis punitur pro eodem delicto - No one can be twice punished for the same offence.

Nemo cogitur suam rem vendere, etiam justo pretio - No one is bound to sell his own property, even for a just price.

Nemo contra factum suum venire potest - No man can contradict his own deed.

Nemo debet esse judex in propria causa - No one can be judge in his own case.

Nemo plus juris transferre ad alium potest quam ipse habet - No one can transfer to another a larger right than he himself has.

Nemo potest contra recordum verificare per patriam - No one can verify by the country, that is, through a jury, against the record.

Nemo potest esse tenens et dominus - No one can at the same time be a tenant and a landlord (of the same tenement).

Nemo potest facere per alium, quod per se non potest - No one can do through another what he cannot do himself.

Nemo potest mutare consilium suum in alterius injuriam - No one can change his purpose to the injury of another.

Nemo praesumitur esse immemor suae aeternae salutis et maxime in articulo mortis - No one is presumed to be forgetful of his eternal welfare, and particularly in the hour of death.

Nemo prohibetur pluribus defensionibus uti - No one is forbidden to make use of several defences.

Nemo punitur pro alieno delicto - No one is punished for the crime of another.

Nemo se accusare debet, nisi coram Deo - No one should accuse himself except in the presence of God.

Nemo tenetur accusare se ipsum nisi coram Deo - No one is bound to accuse himself except in the presence of God.

Nemo tenetur armare adversarium contra se - No one is bound to arm his adversary against himself.

Nexus - Connection

Nihil quod est inconveniens est licitum - Nothing inconvenient is lawful.

Nil facit error nominis cum de corpore constat - An error of name makes not difference when it appears from the body of the instrument.

Nisi - Unless

Non compus mentis - Not of sound mind and understanding

Non constat - It is not certain

Non decipitur qui scit se decipi - He is not deceived who knows that he is deceived.

Non definitur in jure quid sit conatus - What an attempt is, is not defined in law.

Non est arctius vinculum inter homines quam jusjurandum - There is no stronger link among men than an oath.

Non est factum - It is not his deed

Non est informatus - He is not informed.

Non facias malum ut inde veniat bonum - You shall not do evil that good may come of it.

Non jus, sed seisina, facit stipitem - Not right, but seisin makes a stock (from which the inheritance must descend).

Non refert quid notum sit judici si notum non sit in forma judicii - It matters not what is known to the judge if it is not known judicially.

Non sequitur - An inconsistent statement, it does not follow

Nullus commodum capere potest ex sua injuria propria - No one can derive an advantage from his own wrong.

Nullus recedat e curia cancellaria sine remedio - No one should depart from a Court of Chancery without a remedy.

Omne sacramentum debet esse de certa scientia - Every oath ought to be of certain knowledge.

Omnia delicta in aperto leviora sunt - All crimes (committed) in the open are (considered) lighter.

Omnia praesumuntur contra spoliatorem - All things are presumed against a wrongdoer.

Omnis innovatio plus novitate perturbat quam utilitate prodeat - Every innovation disturbs more by its novelty than it benefits by its utility.

Optima legum interpres est consuetudo - The best interpreter of laws is custom.

Optimus interpres rerum est usus - The best interpreter of things is usage.

P

Pacta privata juri publico non derogare possunt - Private contracts cannot derogate from public law.

Par delictum - Equal fault.

Pari passu - On an equal footing.

Partus sequitur ventrem - The offspring follows the mother.

Pater est quem nuptiae demonstrant - The father is he whom the marriage points out.

Peccata contra naturam sunt gravissima - Wrongs against nature are the most serious.

Pendente lite nihil innovetur - During litigation nothing should be changed.

Per curiam - In the opinion of the court.

Per minas - By means of menaces or threats.

Per quod - By reason of which.

Post mortem - After death.

Prima facie - On the face of it.

Prima impressionis - On first impression.

Pro hac vice - For this occasion.

Pro rata - In proportion.

Pro tanto - So far, to that extent.

Pro tempore - For the time being.

Publici juris - Of public right.

Q

Quaeitur - The question is raised.

Quantum - How much, an amount.

Qui facit per alium, facit per se - He who acts through another acts himself.

Qui haeret in litera, haeret in cortice - He who stices to the letter, sticks to the bark.

Qui in utero est, pro jam nato habetur, quoties de ejus commodo quaeritur - He who is in the womb is considered as already born as far as his benefit is considered.

Qui non habet potestatem alienandi, habet necessitatem retinendi - He who has not the power of alienating is under the necessity of retaining.

Qui non habet, ille non dat - He who has not, does not give.

Qui non improbat, approbat - He who does not disapprove, approves.

Qui non obstat quod obstare potest facere videtur - He who does not prevent what he is able to prevent, is considered as committing the thing.

Qui non prohibet quod prohibere potest assentire videtur - He who does not prohibit when he is able to prohibit, is in fault.

Qui peccat ebrius, luat sobrius - He who does wrong when drunk must be punished when sober.

Qui potest et debet vetare et non vetat jubet - He who is able and ought to forbit and does not, commands.

Qui prior est tempore potior est jure - He who is prior in time is stronger in right.

Qui sentit commodum, debet et sentire onus - He who derives a benefit ought also to bear a burden.

Qui tacet consentire videtur - He who is silent appears to consent.

Quid pro quo - Consideration. something for something.

Quidcquid plantatur solo, solo cedit - Whatever is planted in or affixed to the soil, belongs to the soil.

Quod ab initio non valet, in tractu temporis non convalescit - What is not valid in the beginning does not become valid by time.

Quod constat curiae opere testium non indiget - What appears to the Court needs not the help of witnesses.

Quod necessarie intelligitur, id non deest - What is necessarily understood is not wanting.

Quod necessitas cogit, defendit - What necessity forces it justifies.

Quod non apparet, non est - What does not appear, is not.

Quod non habet principium non habet finem - What has no beginning has no end.

Quod per me non possum, nec per alium - What I cannot do through myself, I cannot do through another.

Quod prius est verius est; et quod prius est tempore potius est jure - What is first is more true; and what is prior in time is stronger in law.

Quod vanum et inutile est, lex non requirit - The law does not require what is vain and useless.

Quoties in verbis nulla est ambiguitas, ibi nulla expositio contra verba expressa fienda est - When there is no ambiguity in words, then no exposition contrary to the expressed words is to be made.

R

Ratio est legis anima, mutata legis ratione mutatur et lex - Reason is the soul of the law; when the reason of the law changes the law also is changed.

Re - In the matter of.

Reprobata pecunia leberat solventem - Money refused releases the debtor.

Res - Matter, affair, thing, circumstance.

Res gestae - Things done.

Res integra - A matter untouched (by decision).

Res inter alios acta alteri nocere non debet - Things done between strangers ought not to affect a third person, who is a stranger to the transaction.

Res judicata accipitur pro veritate - A thing adjudged is accepted for the truth.

Res nulis - Nobodys property.

Respondeat superior - Let the principal answer.

Rex est major singulis, minor universis - The King is greater than individuals, less than all the people.

Rex non debet judicare sed secundum legem - The King ought not to judge but according to the law.

Rex non potest peccare - The King can do no wrong.

Rex nunquma moritur - The King never dies.

Rex quod injustum est facere non potest - The King cannot do what is unjust.

S

Salus populi est suprema lex - The safety of the people is the supreme law.

Sciens - Knowingly.

Scienter - Knowingly.

Scire facias - That you cause to know.

Scribere est agere - To write is to act.

Se defendendo - In self defence.

Secus - The legal position is different, it is otherwise.

Semper praesumitur pro legitimatione puerorum - Everything is presumed in favor of the legitimacy of children.

Semper pro matriomonio praesumitur - It is always presumed in favor of marriage.

Sententia interlocutoria revocari potest, definitiva non potest - An interlocutory order can be revoked, a final order cannot be.

Servitia personalia sequuntur personam - Personal services follow the person.

Sic utere tuo ut alienum non laedas - So use your own as not to injure anothers property.

Simplex commendatio non obligat - A simple recommendation does not bind.

Stare decisis - To stand by decisions (precedents).

Stet - Do not delete, let it stand.

Sub modo - Within limits.

Sub nomine - Under the name of.

Sub silentio - In silence.

Sublata causa, tollitur effectus - The cause being removed, the effect ceases.

Sublato fundamento, cadit opus - The foundation being removed, the structure falls.

Subsequens matrimonium tollit peccatum praecedens - A subsequent marriage removes the preceding wrong.

Suggestio falsi - The suggestion of something which is untrue.

Sui generis - Unique.

Summa ratio est quae pro religione facit - The highest reason is that which makes for religion, i.e. religion dictates.

Suppressio veri - The suppression of the truth.

Suppressio veri expressio falsi - A suppression of truth is equivalent to an expression of falsehood.

T

Talis qualis - Such as it is.

Terra firma - Solid ground.

Testamenta latissimam interpretationem habere debent - Testaments ought to have the broadest interpretation.

Traditio loqui chartam facit - Delivery makes a deed speak.

Transit terra cum onere - The land passes with its burden.

U

Ubi eadem ratio ibi idem jus, et de similibus idem est judicium - When there is the same reason, then the law is the same, and the same judgment should be rendered as to similar things.

Ubi jus ibi remedium est - Where there is a right there is a remedy.

Ubi non est principalis, non potest esse accessorius - Where there is no principal, there can be no accessory.

Ubi nullum matrimonium, ibi nulla dos es - Where there is no marriage, there is no dower.

Ultima voluntas testatoris est perimplenda secundum veram intentionem suam - The last will of a testator is to be fulfilled according to his true intentio.

Ut poena ad paucos, metus ad omnes, perveniat - That punishment may come to a few, the fear of it should affect all.

Utile per inutile non vitiatur - What is useful is not vitiated by the useless.

Verba chartarum fortius accipiuntur contra preferentem - The words of deeds are accepted more strongly against the person offering them.

Verba debent intelligi cum effectu - Words ought to be understood with effect.

Verba intentioni, non e contra, debent inservire - Words ought to serve the intention, not the reverse.

Verbatim - Word by word, exactly.

Vi et armis - With the force and arms.

Via antiqua via est tuta - The old way is the safe way.

Vice versa - The other way around.

Vide - See.

Vigilantibus non dormientibus jura subveniunt - The laws serve the vigilant, not those who sleep.

Vir et uxor consentur in lege una persona - A husband and wife are regarded in law as one person.

Visitationem commendamus - We recommend a visitation.

Volens - Willing.

Volenti non fit injuria - An injury is not done to one consenting to it.

Voluntas in delictis non exitus spectatur - In offences the intent and not the result is looked at.

Voluntas reputatur pro facto - The will is taken for the deed.

www.ingramcontent.com/pod-product-compliance
Lightning Source LLC
Chambersburg PA
CBHW051241170526
45165CB00004B/1529